Isabel Quigly

CHARLIE CHAPLIN

early comedies

Studio Vista | Dutton Pictureback

General editor David Herbert

To Crispin

Acknowledgments
I would like to thank the staff of the Stills Section of the
National Film Archive at the British Film Institute and John
Kobal for supplying the stills reproduced in this book. The
pictures on page 148 from Charles Chaplin's *Autobiography*
are reproduced with kind permission of The Bodley Head Ltd.

I. Q.

Published in London by Studio Vista Limited
Blue Star House, Highgate Hill, N19
and in New York by E. P. Dutton and Co Inc
201 Park Avenue South, New York, NY 10003
Distributed in Canada by General Publishing Co Ltd
30 Lesmill Road, Don Mills, Ontario
Set in 8D on 9 pt Univers, 2 pt leaded
Made and printed in Great Britain by
Richard Clay (The Chaucer Press) Ltd
Bungay, Suffolk

SBN 289 37021 3 (paperback)
SBN 289 37023 x (hardback)

Contents

The legend

The trouble with being a legend in your own lifetime is that you are quickly barnacled with other legends. The stories, if repeated often enough, become sacrosanct; a theory, a suggestion or an interpretation, the vaguest notion of the woolliest commentator, tends to solidify, be repeated, quoted, and in no time at all turn into cliché. Almost before you realize it you are encrusted with the ideas of others, interpreted out of the everyday world into one of words, metaphors, symbols.

So much has been written (and overwritten) about Chaplin that it sometimes feels like clawing through cottonwool before you reach his creation, Charlie. (Charlie and Chaplin, incidentally, are not at all the same person, which is what makes Chaplin's auto-biography so disconcerting: you expect to find Charlie in it and instead meet someone who often seems totally different, at times almost incompatible with him.) Most of what has been written is both as true and as untrue as any cliché: which means as un-helpful. Endlessly repeated phrases like 'little man', 'tragic clown', 'immortal tramp', besides making one squirm a bit, have been used too often to make any impact. They may be true enough, but they are wasted. They are his barnacles, the inevitable stiffeners and concealers of anyone famous, certainly of anyone legendary.

And it all happened so quickly, it was like the overnight fame of a present-day pop-star. Chaplin was probably the first enter-tainer to get what is now their familiar treatment: Charlie became a cartoon character, kicking and bouncing his way about the comic strips, and very early in his career he was used in the kind of 'novelty' now sold to promote anything and anyone, but in those days something really new. By the middle of 1915, *Photo-play Magazine* was advertising

> '*Now only* $1.00
> *12 Inch Statuette of* **Charles Chaplin**
> *The Newest Fad*
> *The country has gone mad about these genuine Charlie Chaplin Statuettes.*'

Very quickly, too, he was found in songs and jingles and—probably more lastingly—in children's games:

> 'One, two, three, four,
> Charlie Chaplin went to war . . .'

they sang in the First World War.
or:
> 'For the moon shines bright on Charlie Chaplin,
> His shoes are cracking,
> For want of blacking,
> And his little baggy trousers want mendin'
> Before they send him
> To the Dardanelles.'

(The original song that inspired this one, a soldiers' song with mildly obscene interpretations, is echoed, incidentally, in *The Waste Land*.)
And children threw a ball against a wall to:

> 'Don't forget to give it to Mary
> And not to Charlie Chaplin.'

All over the world he was given local names—Charlot, Carlito; his physique belonged nowhere, therefore everywhere. He was called —not too ridiculously then; and not too ridiculously even now, which shows how the legend has lasted—the most famous human being since Jesus Christ.

At a more highbrow level, he transcended frontiers in all directions—in time and space and, as it were, in sympathy. The most disparate sorts of acclaim came to him, quite suddenly. His face was said to be 'in the pure French tradition . . . subtle, ironic, sentimentally sensual, acute and unheeding'. It was compared

with the faces drawn by Japanese artists, or those of Velasquez, Dürer, the Flemish primitives. Young, it was said to resemble that of Keats, old, that of Yeats. Charlie was compared with innumerable fictional or mythical characters, sad or comic or both; with Pan and Pierrot and Pagliacci, Sir Galahad, Don Juan and Faust, with Chaucer's 'verray parfit gentil knight', with Hamlet, Cyrano de Bergerac, Don Quixote and Brer Rabbit; with people who really lived—outcasts like Villon, social rebels like Byron or Rimbaud or Baudelaire, saints like Francis of Assisi; and with practically every great mime or clown in history—Deburau, Grimaldi, Dan Leno, Raimu—as well as his greatest contemporary in what might be called plastic self-expression—Nijinsky. Everything and everyone seemed to recall him, he seemed universally applicable.

Thus Charlie, created by Chaplin, answered a need that seemed universal. If he hadn't existed, you feel, he would have had to be invented. Being filled with contradictions (elegance and penury, grace and clumsiness, toughness and pathos, cheek and misfortune) he belonged everywhere and nowhere. Being silent, he could speak to anyone. So he was recognized at once: not just in the sense that he was taken to people's hearts but in a more literal sense. Though he looked outlandish, he seemed familiar, a person people recognized as if they had seen him before, someone so basic that he summed up all sorts of basic reactions, wishes and ideas. And in the sense that the feelings he conjured were familiar, the mixture of amusement and sadness was universal, he *had* been known before.

11

Every popular fictional character, from Mr Pickwick to Mickey Mouse, is either a type or a symbol. The type simply repeats what others have been like before it, is just an agglomeration of attributes; the symbol sums up in itself all kinds of ideas and fantasies and influences. The type narrows everything to its own limitations and so deadens imagination, whereas the symbol fires it, being open to anything and everything. In Chaplin's case Charlie was so much of a symbol—so broadly applicable, as it were, to life all over the place, so universally appealing—that his own creator was not consciously aware of it all, and looked on the character he had suddenly brought forth ('on the spur of a few horror-stricken moments', according to Robert Payne) with a kind of fascinated respect, unsure what he might get up to and what he implied, how far he would go; how far, above all, he would go *from Chaplin.*

Chaplin was, in a sense, possessed by Charlie and, like most artists *vis-à-vis* their creations, could not really explain him, let alone the way he came into being, in a rational way. Admittedly he was a meticulous artist, careful and tireless in planning, getting and perfecting his effects: there was nothing slapdash about anything he did, nothing casual, fortuitous or merely lucky in its results. All the same, it is perfectly clear from the way he has talked about him that Chaplin did not encompass the whole of Charlie, that Charlie, as it were, took charge and dictated how he was to behave, and that there would always be mysteries about him which Chaplin could never explain, actions he could not foresee. Always he referred to his creation objectively, from the outside—as 'Charlie' and as 'he'; 'without familiarity and with enormous respect', again according to Payne. 'Even then,' Chaplin said much later, about Charlie's first appearance at the very end of 1913, in a five-minute film called *Kid auto races in Venice*, released the following February, 'I realized I would have to spend the rest of my life finding out more about the creature.

Kid auto races in Venice

The evolution of the famous moustache

For me he was fixed, complete, the moment I looked in the mirror and saw him for the first time, yet even now I don't know all the things that are to be known about him.' 'I created him,' he said on another occasion, 'but I am not him, and yet sometimes our paths cross.'

Of course, one can suspect a pinch of hindsight in this, a certain retrospective response, as it were, to all that had been written and elaborated about Charlie since he came into being. The creation of Charlie has been analysed so often and so minutely that it would be odd if Chaplin were not, to some extent, inclined to nod agreement with at least some of it. But his feelings at the time were probably less complex and less selfconscious than they became with time, fame and highbrow analysis. His description of the birth of Charlie, in his autobiography, is almost disconcertingly straightforward : 'I had no idea what make-up to put on. I did not like my get-up as the press reporter. However, on the way to the wardrobe I thought I would dress in baggy pants, big shoes, a cane and a derby hat. I wanted everything a contradiction : the pants baggy, the coat tight, the hat small and the shoes large. I was undecided whether to look old or young, but remembering Sennett had expected me to be a much older man, I added a small moustache, which, I reasoned, would add age without hiding my expression.

'I had no idea of the character. But the moment I was dressed,

the clothes and the make-up made me feel the person he was. I began to know him, and by the time I walked on to the stage he was fully born.'

'The surprising and beautiful thing,' Robert Payne commented on this, 'was that all these odds and ends fitted together. They formed a new character whose possibilities Chaplin only half understood, though he was to explore them at length. The character had emerged suddenly, fully formed.'

But the story of Charlie's background and first appearance has been told much more elaborately. In another account Chaplin himself makes Charlie seem more cerebral and deliberate:

'I didn't know what sort of comic character I could take up,' he writes. 'But after a little I thought of all these little Englishmen I had seen with their little black moustaches, their tight clothes and their bamboo canes, and I fixed on these as my model.'

The ancestry of every bit of his costume has, of course, been explained and analysed. The huge trousers were Fatty Arbuckle's, and so was the bowler hat, which was slightly small on Charlie, and 'balanced gravely, like a yacht on water'. The enormous shoes, with their long, curled-up toes, were the comedian Ford Sterling's, but the inspiration for the way Charlie walked in them was an old cabman in Kennington Road, who shuffled along because his feet were painful. Whole chapters have been written on the significance of these pathetic, earthbound, monstrous

15

Making a living with Virginia Kirtley, Alice Davenport

shoes, weighing down the soaring spirit within them : as Chaplin himself put it, 'The little chap I want to show wears the air of romantic hunger, is forever seeking romance, but his feet won't let him.'

The cane Chaplin called 'perhaps my best find,' although at first he was hardly aware that 'for millions of individuals, a walking-stick marks a man as rather a "swell".' This was exactly what was wanted, a solemn, dignified adjunct to the costume, capable of any amount of 'business'. The moustache, it is generally supposed, was painted on ; yet as early as 1915 the contradictory legend was already being put about that Chaplin had gradually trimmed off the long, rather Chinese-looking 'villain' moustache he had worn in his first film, *Making a living*, together with an unmemorable and thoroughly un-Charlieish costume consisting of frock coat, tall hat and monocle.

Charlie may have been born full-grown—'a tramp, a gentleman, a poet, a dreamer, a lonely fellow, always hopeful of romance and adventure', as Chaplin says he described him to Mack Sennett the moment he put on the costume. But in *Kid auto races* and the other films (thirty-five, no less) made during 1914, his year with Sennett at the Keystone Studios, Charlie was a simpler, more slapstick character than he was later to become : as the late G. W. Stonier put it : 'The wonderfully haunting mask is what has grown on Charlie with the years.' In the Keystone films he was, as a rule, an engagingly 'bad' character : 'he would have you believe he is a scientist, a musician, a duke, a polo-player', Chaplin told Sennett. 'However, he is not above picking up cigarette-butts or robbing a baby of its candy. And, of course, if the occasion warrants it, he will kick a lady in the rear !' It was this blundering, anarchical side of Charlie that appeared in the films turned out at an astonishing speed during that first year, improvised on the spot. The 'pale, god-like figure' that was the total Charlie was implicit in this early character, but for the present it was lying low.

Keystone Studios

It was in December 1913 that the twenty-four-year-old Chaplin arrived at Mack Sennett's Keystone Studios. 'Mr Sennett was shocked to see how young I looked,' he has written.' ''I thought you were a much older man,'' he said. I could detect a tinge of concern, which made me anxious, remembering that all Sennett's comedians were oldish-looking men . . . ''I can make up as old as you like,'' I answered.' It was a wretchedly uncertain beginning to his film career: 'For days I wandered around the studio, wondering when I would start work. Occasionally I would meet Sennett crossing the stage, but he would look through me, preoccupied. I had an uncomfortable feeling that he thought he had made a mistake in engaging me.' Later, Sennett said: 'I don't know why I did it. I wasn't too hopeful.'

Sennett had first seen Chaplin when he was playing a drunk in *A night in an English music hall* in Fred Karno's company, touring the States and Canada and, when Sennett saw it, playing in New York. 'If I ever become a big shot, there's a guy I'll sign up,' Sennett said—but as he was then working as a five-dollar-a-day extra for D. W. Griffith in the Biograph Company, the chance seemed pretty remote. It was on Chaplin's second visit to America, in Philadelphia, that a telegram came to the company manager. 'I wonder if this means you,' he said to Chaplin. The telegram ran: 'Is there a man named Chaffin in your company or something like that stop if so will he communicate with Kessell and Bauman, 24 Longacre Building Broadway.' Chaplin dreamed of an inheritance from some unknown rich aunt; but the reality—Sennett's offer of a contract—was surprising enough. The money ($150 a week for the first three months, $175 after that: a fortune, it seemed to him) and the publicity value of working in the already famous Keystone comedies, tempted Chaplin; he recalled thinking: 'A year at that racket and I could return to vaudeville an international star.' Yet he was dubious, and when he reached the Keystone Studios his doubts increased. The Keystone comedies he considered: 'a crude mélange of rough and tumble', Sennett told him: 'We get an idea then follow the natural sequence of events until it leads to a chase, which is the essence of our comedy'; upon which Chaplin remarks: 'Personally I hated a chase. It dissipates personality; little as I knew about movies, I knew that nothing transcended personality.'

After days of loafing, apparently unwanted, about the studios, a film was made at last, in three days. Sennett's second-in-command, Harry Lehrman, directed and (according to Chaplin, at least) afterwards cut out any possible merit it might have had, just to cut Chaplin down to size. *Making a living* had Chaplin (not yet Charlie) playing an Englishman down on his luck, and determined to retrieve it, a sharper, a cad; and although the *Moving Picture World* described him as 'a comedian of the first water', Chaplin himself said of the film: 'It broke my heart, for the cutter had butchered it beyond recognition, cutting into the middle of all my funny business.' Certainly it makes no particular impression today: the bouncing 'toff' character has only the slightly weird historical interest of being played by the (barely recognizable) creator of Charlie.

'Nothing transcended personality,' Chaplin passionately believed, and his belief was justified in the most unlikely film, made some time—no one knows the exact day—during the last week of that frustrating December 1913, in only 45 minutes; a film that turned out to be so short it shared a single reel with a documentary on olive oil. *Kid auto races at Venice* had no story and absolutely no pretentions or high hopes: it just showed a man getting in the way of the camera that was taking pictures at a children's car race. But the man was Charlie; not Charlie in all his fullness and richness—that was to grow gradually—but the tough, obstreperous, anarchical Charlie that was at least half of the later whole; a Charlie who dashed in and out of the film determined to undermine the authority of cops and photographers, mocking the children who shot down the middle of the street in their wooden cars, alternately flouting authority and helping the police to shove the crowd behind ropes at the street side, exploding with rage and with laughter, with fun and frustration.

What is remarkable about this brief first appearance of Charlie's is not just the amount of character it managed to cram into the space of a very few minutes, but the immediate effectiveness and richness of Charlie's presence. A simple comic part is easy enough to make instantly effective: the actor plays something easily labelled—fat man, stooge, bully, victim—and the audience knows just how to react to him, just what is expected of it: approval indulgence, hisses, support. A complex part, like that of Charlie, is very much harder to put across effectively in a short space of time, because the audience doesn't have this immediate, pat response, doesn't really know how to take him.

There is a kind of Charlieolatry that suggests Charlie's universality is so complete that *everybody* responds to him, is won over, amused, touched, carried away: in fact, this is not the case at all. Charlie occasionally arouses strong feelings of prejudice and dislike (though never, it would seem, of boredom), sometimes in those who try to reconcile the figure of Charlie with the 'real' Chaplin, and fail to, sometimes in those on whom, as a personality, Charlie quite simply grates. Or perhaps it is not as simple as all that. For within the character of Charlie himself there is a duality that makes him, for all his instant appeal to many, suspect and difficult to others. He is, as it were, on both sides of every situation, therefore rather ambiguous towards the audience, and sometimes ambiguously reacted to: he is both victim and bully, both under-dog and obstreperous, both innocent and sly, both romantic and sensual. Then the 'little man' aspect of the character, stressed by Chaplin himself (who uses the word 'little' a great deal in writing about Charlie), but in fact only a part of it, irritates some; and the mythology that has surrounded his figure from the start, the way he became the intellectuals' darling overnight, probably irritates others.

Appealing or not, there is no doubt of his effectiveness from the start. The odd thing is, Mack Sennett failed to see it. Even several films later he was prepared to sack Chaplin because he could not agree with Mabel Normand, his leading lady and at first, absurdly, the so-called director of some of their films. Only a telegram from the New York office, urging Sennett to hurry up with some more Chaplin pictures, to satisfy the sudden demand for them, saved Chaplin his job.

Mabel's strange predicament with Harry McCoy

Mabel's strange predicament was Chaplin's third, and Charlie's second, film, the one that began to make people sit up and ask who he was. Mabel Normand was then Keystone's chief actress, and described by Chaplin as the justification for the existence of the Keystone comedies. 'She was extremely pretty,' he wrote, 'with large, heavy-lidded eyes and full lips that curled delicately at the corners of her mouth, expressing humour and all sorts of indulgence. She was light-hearted and gay, a good fellow, kind and generous; and everyone adored her.' She was also, when set over Chaplin as director of her own pictures, a difficulty. 'Sweet Mabel,' Chaplin wrote, 'at that time she was only twenty, pretty and charming, everybody's favourite, everybody loved her': she was also in love with Sennett and might have got Chaplin out of films if the first few times he appeared had not already found him an audience.

There was nothing in the action of *Mabel's strange predicament* except chases in and out of hotel rooms, with a husband, a lover, and Charlie as the hotel gate-crasher. Here the mannerisms that were to become so characteristic—the outsize dignity preserved at all costs, the gesture of absurd delicacy in unsuitable situations—began to appear. In the hotel lobby, Charlie tripped over a lady's foot and raised his hat to apologize; then tripped over a cuspidor, and did the same. It was after making this film that Chaplin, seeing the reactions of the studio crowd—stage-hands, carpenters, people from the wardrobe department, actors from other films—felt that he had made good, and decided to stick to the Charlie costume at all costs. On the way home after the day's filming a small-part actor told him: 'Boy, you've started something.'

Pages 24–25
Mabel's strange predicament with Harry McCoy

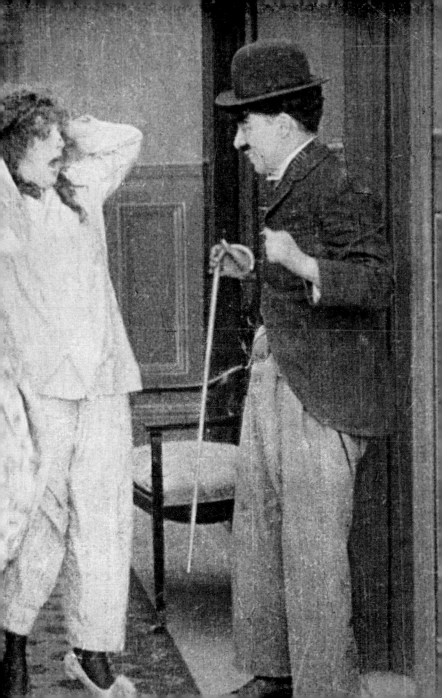

The end of Sennett's contract

So, for a year, he was Sennett's man at Keystone, and Charlie developed his range, his film sense and the mannerisms that so quickly became famous, but not (for the time being, at least) his character or his presence, which in any case were strangely and satisfactorily complete from the moment Chaplin put on the hat, moustache and shoes. He raised his hat straight up off his head (as you still see jokey elderly men do sometimes today, surely in imitation—conscious or unconscious—of Chaplin), he did miraculous things with doors, windows and cupboards, with anything that opened and shut and provided an entrance, an exit or a refuge, he used inanimate objects to splendid comic effect by treating them as they were not used to being treated—more respectfully and ceremoniously, as a rule, so that the whole world around him echoed the incongruity of his down-at-heel toff's dress, the basic absurdity of a tramp sporting cane and bowler.

It was a case of the Keystone comedies on the one hand, and Charlie on the other, coming together and to some extent compromising, so that Charlie added immeasurably to the comedies and they, to some extent, limited his development. But it was a good film apprenticeship, as Fred Karno's company had been the best training ground for his particular gifts of mime and satire. The Keystone comedies depended on plenty of simple, energetic 'business'—furiously fast goings-on, chases, confusions, pie-throwing, misunderstandings, incongruities, failures of recognition, mistaken identities, explosions and uproars, social chaos of every kind. Broad and exuberant though they were, developing spontaneously, as it were, out of the landscape (as the famous Keystone cops developed out of a few shots of some *real* policemen who happened to run into one of the films and looked funnier than anyone else around), their mixture of farce and slapstick was essentially cinematic, a matter of movement and contrast, and never something static and stagey. The films were improvised on the spot, often more like charades than anything else ; but Chaplin,

A busy day with Mack Swain

A busy day

who at twenty-four already had about seventeen years' professional experience, on and off, behind him, was never anything but wholly professional.

The figure of Charlie, in contrast with this furious activity, from the first was subtle and suggestive and disturbing, full of an individuality that might, had it not been so strong, have been lost in the Keystone preposterousness and excitement. Always it was cleft down the middle : on the one hand, in these early films especially, there was the figure that came straight from Chaplin's childhood, a time of what now seems incredible poverty, deprivation and precocious suffering ; on the other, the fastidious, hat-raising, down-on-his-luck, diminutive toff. Mostly the first side won : Charlie was a pretty tough character in his Keystone days, often, in fact, the official villain of the piece ; in any case he was likelier to fight back than to look pathetic, invincibly cheeky towards fate or his enemies, invariably fertile in thinking up ways to daunt the opposition or cover a mistake. Perpetually at odds with society, he was never quite overwhelmed by it ; longing for romance—more precisely, for Mabel Normand—he never quite found it (or her). He was strangely ageless and disconcertingly agile, with a dancer's body on those elephantine trousers and feet, and a youngster's pale, sad face behind the disguising moustache.

At Keystone Charlie had any number of jobs and roles, while remaining himself ; just occasionally Chaplin took over, in the cause of versatility, and played someone else—a rich man foiled in his suicide attempts, in *Cruel, cruel love,* or a tough wife who caught her husband flirting with another woman, in *A busy day.* In *Mabel at the wheel* he wore his frock coat and tall hat again, in *The masquerader* he was an actor who dressed up as a woman (and seems remarkably, undatedly attractive at this distance, in contrast to many of the actresses of the time, whose charm it is hard to see fifty years later). In the other films his jobs varied : in *His musical career* he was a piano mover, dragging the wrong pianos up and down and finally into a lake, in *Dough and dynamite* a dexterous baker, flourily bashing at Chester Conklin or flipping circular doughnuts off his wrist ; in *The property man* he was a work-shy prop-man, in *The knockout* a boxing referee ; in *Her friend the bandit* a bandit posing as a count (as was several times

Dough and Dynamite

Dough and dynamite

to happen later) in order to get to a party, in *Caught in a cabaret* a waiter, posing once more as someone grand enough to be invited to Mabel Normand's party. In *The new janitor* he was the janitor of an office building, with mop and pail (to drop on the boss below) and weary climbs upstairs; in *Laughing gas* he was some sort of

The property man

unspecified stooge to Dr Pain, the dentist, counting patients, emptying cuspidors, tapping an unconscious patient on the head with a mallet, fetching a prescription and stopping on the way to admire and alarm the dentist's wife, and flirting outrageously when at last he got a pretty patient into the chair.

Caught in a cabaret with Mabel Normand

Laughing gas

Laughing gas with Joseph Swickard

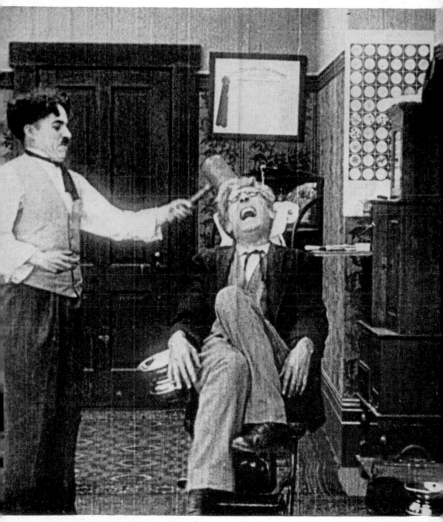

But mostly he was Charlie in this or that situation, more or less tramp-like (sometimes more, sometimes less), raising uproar and confusion. In *A film Johnnie* he invaded the Keystone studios and caused chaos among the film-makers; in *Tango tangles* he made similar chaos in a (real life) dance-hall. Landladies and girls in the park, the only women a poor man might be expected to meet,

A film Johnnie

were the main objects of his fancy; drink and a taste for general mayhem the main causes of disaster. Often there was comic byplay between Charlie and one or other of the Keystone comedians— Ford Sterling, Chester Conklin, Mack Swain, the endearing Fatty Arbuckle, whose vast trousers he first used for the Charlie costume. In *Between showers* he and Ford Sterling both tried to help a stout

Between showers with Emma Clifton, Ford Sterling, Chester Conklin

girl across a puddle; in *Twenty minutes of love*, he and Chester Conklin were competing for the same girl; in *The fatal mallet* everyone was after Mabel, who behaved haughtily; in *Those love pangs* it was a case of both landlady *and* girls in the park, with Charlie and Chester Conklin pursuing both; in *His trysting place* Charlie was actually married to Mabel, with a baby he yanked up

Between showers with Emma Clifton, Ford Sterling, Chester Conklin

by the scruff of its pants, in a now famously untender grip, and lots of confusion over the wrong overcoat and the wrong love-letter found in its pocket, and again more uproar and sorting-out in the park; in *Getting acquainted*, at a tremendous pace, and with enormously skilful timing, there was more marital confusion in the park.

Twenty minutes of love

His trysting place with Mabel Normand

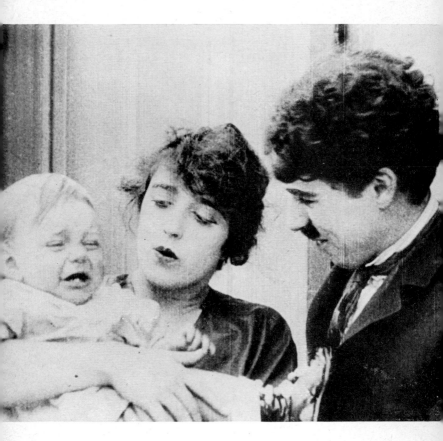

His trysting place

Getting acquainted with Mabel Normand

The face on the bar-room floor

Mabel's busy day

Mabel's busy day with Mabel Normand

Recreation

As the lodging-house was home to Charlie, so the park was his stamping-ground, source of adventure and girls and thrills, at once his social centre and the constant reminder of his loneliness and social limitations. On his first visit to London after becoming famous, Chaplin visited his old haunts in Kennington and sat on a park bench, remembering his first love, Hetty, and his nineteen-year-old self waiting for her there. 'How depressing to me are all parks!' he wrote after this visit. 'The loneliness of them. One never goes to a park unless one is lonesome. And lonesomeness is sad. The symbol of sadness, that's a park.' The symbol of sadness, perhaps, in certain moods, but also the source of what social life a character like Charlie could hope for, with the chance of romance just around the next bush, if only you knew where to look for it.

1914 was a year of almost incredible fertility for Chaplin, with films pouring out every few days, made in a few days, sometimes in a few hours. After three or four months at Keystone he started directing and writing his own films: the first he made entirely on his own was *Caught in the rain*, about a sleep-walking lady and a large jealous husband, played by Mack Swain. Of the thirty-five he made that year, about twenty-two were under his direction, though occasionally he shared the directing honours with Mabel Normand. The method of making these films was splendidly haphazard, wild and inspirational, and it made everything seem an adventure; someone might say: 'There's a flood down town on Main Street,' and there would be an idea for a Keystone comedy. 'It was this charming alfresco spirit that was a delight,' Chaplin wrote much later, 'a challenge to one's creativeness.' 'In those early movies,' he said, 'I knew I had many advantages, and that, like a geologist, I was entering a rich unexplored field. I suppose that was the most exciting period of my career, for I was on the threshold of something wonderful.'

It was in the middle of these high jinks with buckets, pails, pies and all sorts of inanimate enemies and allies, that Chaplin first realized—consciously, that is—his own ability to bring tears as well as laughter to an audience. During the making of *The new janitor* he had to mime, for the benefit of the office manager, who was firing him for his clumsiness, the large number of children he had to provide for, and an elderly actress watching him found herself in tears. 'I know it's supposed to be funny, but you just make me weep,' she told him, confirming something he had already felt, though not formulated, and certainly something that was a basic part of Charlie's appeal.

The new janitor

All the Keystone comedies but one were short—one- or two-reel-ers. The exception, a feature-length comedy, was *Tillie's punctured romance*, which was quite unlike the impromptu incidents round which the other comedies were built because it had a story, a script, a beginning, an end and something of a middle, and was based on a musical comedy. It was a burlesque of the old tale of the innocent country girl and the cad, with the large and formidable Marie Dressler, of all people, playing the maiden, as she had done on the stage, and Mabel Normand, naturally enough, as the other woman

Tillie's punctured romance with Marie Dressler (*and opposite*)

Getting acquainted with Phyllis Allen, Mabel Normand, Mack
Swain

The masquerader with Vivian Edwards, Cecile Arnold

The rounders with Roscoe (Fatty) Arbuckle

The rounders with Roscoe (Fatty) Arbuckle

with whom Charlie, having fleeced Tillie, heartlessly bolted. Tillie was a farm-girl whose money set Charlie the cad up in urban style, and whom he quickly deserted when the chance came; she took a job as a waitress when he left her penniless, and met him again in the restaurant; but later, when she inherited a fortune from her uncle, he couldn't wait to get his hands on it and her again. The films had plenty of familiar Keystone business, wild chases, kicks, the Keystone cops, a ballroom scene full of angry gunfire and a love-scene between Tillie and Charlie on a high fence. In the end Charlie was left high and dry by both women, who were left to comfort each other with the wry realization that: 'He ain't no good to neither of us!'

His prehistoric past

Chaplin's last film for Keystone was *His prehistoric past,* proto-type of the other film dreams in which Charlie the tramp was transferred to some imaginative existence far from the squalid present. On the familiar park bench ('symbol of sadness') he lay and slept himself into prehistory, where he wore an animal's skin but still kept on his bowler hat, and where he overcame his enemy King Lowbrow (played by Mack Swain) and marched over the bodies of the king's maidens. Then the king rose again and knocked him on the head, and Charlie woke to find a policeman looming over him. 'All I need to make a comedy is a park, a policeman and a pretty girl,' he told Sennett, and his last Keystone film, like so many of the others, proved him right.

His prehistoric past with Mack Swain

Essanay

Astonishingly (it now seems), Sennett did not renew Chaplin's contract. They could not agree on terms, and Sennett thought Chaplin was asking too much: $1000 a week, more than he was getting himself. So, after some hesitation, a few weeks without offers from elsewhere, and thoughts of setting up on his own (his brother Sydney, then with the Keystone company himself and soon to be Chaplin's business manager, was not enthusiastic, however, at the idea of anything so risky), he went to the Essanay company, which signed him up for $1250 a week, nearly ten times what Sennett had paid him a year before, and a starting bonus of $10,000, all of which he had difficulty in collecting, at least at first. The first of his fourteen Essanay films, which were made during the whole of 1915 and the first weeks of 1916, was made in Chicago, the rest were made in California; Chaplin wrote and directed them all himself, in spite of what he described as the Essanay practice of dealing out scripts like playing cards on Monday mornings.

His new job *opposite:* with Charlotte Mineau

At Keystone he had become technically expert in film-making, and used to the particular Keystone techniques of improvisation, speed and simplicity. Sennett had not used studio scenery and props and arranged interiors: he liked outdoor scenes in parks or other real places, with sunshine instead of studio lighting, he made films fast and cheaply, he liked jokes to be simple and immediate in their impact, he invented funny policemen and the custard pie. Charlie, who appeared so strangely complete from the start, whose personality seemed formed with mysterious suddenness the moment he took over Chaplin, did not really develop any further

His new job

in those first twelve months of his existence: everything was in him already, latent if not yet apparent to everyone, the pathos and sadness as well as the wit, agility, balletic movement, cheek, malice, unexpectedness. But it took the subtler, more self-conscious methods of Essanay film-making to bring all this out.

Without straining critical terms too far, the Essanay films can be called Chaplin's 'middle period', because they really spanned the space (technically, emotionally, intellectually, in the development of Charlie as well as in the development of Chaplin the film-maker) between the lighthearted Keystone films and his great period of

Pages 60–61 **A night out** with Ben Turpin, Leo White
His new job with Ben Turpin

Mutual films from 1916–17, when he was at his height. Chaplin realized, of course, the pot-holes of selfconsciousness and even pretentiousness that lay in wait for him as soon as he abandoned the simple, satisfactory, but limiting Keystone formula. These pot-holes mostly concerned the nature of Charlie himself, the development of relationships and personalities within the framework of slapstick comedy. 'In the Keystone comedies,' he wrote, 'the tramp had been freer and less confined to plot. His brain was seldom active then—only his instincts, which were concerned with the basic essentials : food, warmth and shelter. But with each succeeding comedy the tramp was growing more complex. Sentiment was beginning to percolate through the character. This became a problem because he was bound by the limits of slapstick. This may sound pretentious, but slapstick demands a most exacting psychology.'

In his Keystone days, Chaplin's response to this demand had been, to some extent, an instinctive one. For all his natural melancholy and his instinctive wish to keep himself to himself, he could hardly fail to be buoyed up into a kind of optimism by the brash jollity of Keystone life. Sennett taught him to follow his nose, when it came to improvising comedy ; to have confidence in his own judgement. 'My means of contriving comedy plot was simple,' he wrote. 'It was the process of getting people in and out of trouble.' When he left Keystone, and Sennett, and the talented professionals he was used to, and found himself in the (at first) unsympathetic atmosphere of Essanay, his judgement seemed, for a few weeks, at least, to fail him. The buoyancy and fun of Keystone was replaced by a rather laboured funniness, and even a certain self-consciousness began to appear. Some of the satire now seems hefty. Of course there were splendid moments in these early Essanay films—Chaplin could hardly have breathed without producing a few of them : pantomime surprises, delicate feats of suggestion and inventiveness—but in spite of them they lacked some of the spontaneity and charm of their rougher Keystone predecessors, and had not yet replaced it with anything very different in kind.

The first five films Chaplin made for Essanay were still very much in the Keystone manner, in fact they often repeated themes and incidents he had used in the Keystone films. *A night out* had more or less the same theme as *The bounders*—two drunken cronies out on the razzle; *The champion* was something like *The knockout*, though with Charlie as the fighter instead of Fatty Arbuckle; *In the park* was a kind of rehash of all sorts of pictures in parks, where girls appeared suddenly to be rescued or fallen in love with, and Charlie clearly spent a large part of his life hanging about in the hope that they would. *His new job*, the only film made in Chicago

The champion with Edna Purviance

had Charlie at his old task of making chaos, again (as in *A film Johnnie*) in a film studio. As the carpenter's mate he created confusion with planks, ladders and the leading lady's train, which he trod on at a crucial moment; then, taking over from the star, he found himself dressed as a kind of Ruritanian hussar, but in spite of a formidable *shako* reached only to the other actors' shoulders. *The Jitney elopement* had him carrying Edna Purviance off in a Ford car, with another suitor in hot pursuit and policemen sprouting, Keystone-style, up from everywhere.

The funniest of these five is *The champion*, in which Charlie shared the honours with a dog as melancholy and dignified as himself, as he was later, even more bravely, to share them with a child. Down and out, Charlie and his dog went looking for a job in a boxing gym. Much was made of Charlie's puny figure, and of the contrast between the enormous gloves he put on and what looked

The champion *below and opposite*

like his matchstick arms. The world fifty years ago seems to have been full of huge fierce moustachioed men who glared and roared their way through it. But Charlie defeated them with superior cunning : inside the right glove he hid a horse-shoe, and with its prodigious whacking power impressed everyone, and at last defeated his gigantic rival in the ring.

At this distance these first Essanay films may look disappointing, but at the time they were winning Chaplin fame and fortune at a remarkable rate. When a New York company offered him $25,000

The Jitney elopement with Paddy McGuire, Lloyd Bacon, Edna Purviance, Fred Goodwins

for a quarter of an hour's appearance nightly for two weeks, Essanay paid him the same sum to keep him away from it; when a new method of distribution meant that his films, still one- and two-reelers, were making unprecedentedly huge sums from the cinemas, he got a $10,000 bonus for each picture. As the end of his contract with Essanay approached, he was offered $350,000 for twelve two-reel pictures, with Essanay paying their production costs; but before signing anything Chaplin demanded $150,000 down—which ended the talks with Essanay. Fifty years ago these

The Jitney elopement with Fred Goodwins, Paddy McGuire, Lloyd Bacon

were astronomical sums; within about three years Chaplin was more or less a millionaire. Fame came as quickly as riches. Sydney gave up acting to devote himself to his brother's finances. Even the girls in the Ziegfeld Follies wore moustaches and bowler hats, big shoes and baggy trousers.

Chaplin's *Autobiography* is as interesting for what it leaves out as for what it says. It does not even mention *The tramp*, which was a turning point in his career. Here, for the first time, appeared the Charlie who is now best remembered: the poet, the dreamer, the pathetic, slighted, joyful, sorrowful, many-sided vagabond. Also

The Jitney elopement with Edna Purviance, Leo White

for the first time, it had a sad ending, a tender atmosphere, a romantic involvement with a girl, as opposed to the mere slapstick cavortings and calf-loves of the earlier films. It was Chaplin's first great film, still two reels long and made in three weeks, but worked upon by Chaplin the perfectionist, who would toil with unwearied patience to achieve exactly the right effect in the most unrehearsed-looking way, and in this film rehearsed some of the small scenes fifty times over.

The tramp had Charlie, of course, playing himself at his most Charlieish, no longer disguised as baker, piano-shifter, lodger or

The tramp

Pages 72–73 **A night at the show**

The tramp with Edna Purviance

otherwise useful member of society but undisguised and free, the essential vagabond, roaming the countryside because that was his nature, not his misfortune. Chaplin got the idea from talking to a tramp he met in San Francisco and gave a meal to, who told him about life on the road, its joys and hungers, its total enjoyment of freedom and irresponsibility. There is something ironic about Chaplin, whose fame rested entirely on his intuitive knowledge—rather than actual experience—of tramphood, questioning a real live tramp, of whom Charlie was, in a sense, the prototype. It conjures up a picture of Ian Fleming buttonholing a spy to get ideas for James Bond.

Charlie the tramp saved Edna, the farmer's daughter, from thieves, and when he was wounded by them she nursed him for a blissful interlude of rest and tenderness and farm work. Then her real lover came home again and Charlie, seeing the end of his idyll, packed up his bundle and set off down a long road into the distance. Other films were to end this way. A lesser man than Chaplin, a lesser tramp than Charlie, would simply have gone off in round-shouldered sorrow as far as the horizon, fading out into pathos; but here the tramp, after walking sadly away for a while, suddenly kicked up his heels and danced off into the distance, tramp-like and joyful and free again.

Charlie the tramp was, in a real sense, not only literally but figuratively born in *The tramp*. Before it he had been Charlie the urchin, the underdog, the fighter-back, the tough, the irresistibly funny; but the Charlie of legend, the Charlie who goes beyond comic business to become a legendary character, the Charlie of pathos and renunciation, of glorious, lyrical freedom, was first found in this very simple tale which in spite of its simplicity was not an incident but a proper story, with a rounded, satisfactory development. Of course there was plenty of the old Charlie about it—that was the best thing about Chaplin at every stage, that he never gave up funny business for pathos, but played the two side by side. The scene in which he pumps the cow's tail up and down to get milk ranks with any of the memorable Keystone moments, such as the time when he fell over the bannisters and landed right way up, still calmly smoking, or the time he hung his hat on his shoe, to cover a hole in the sole of it.

The bank with Edna Purviance

Of the other Essanay comedies, *The bank* is outstanding, and probably the most popular and the best known Chaplin film of this period as well. Again Chaplin played a man rejected in love, covering a wider range of feeling than he had done in *The tramp*, suffering more tragically at the end, clowning more furiously at the beginning. Again (as at Keystone) he played an office janitor;

again he did mad things with mops and buckets, outraging the feelings and the faces of innumerable important people, including the manager, customers and his fellow-janitor. Again, as ever, he was in love with an unattainable girl, this time the typist, as always played by Edna Purviance. Again as in *His prehistoric past*, a dream took him out of the drab present into unspeakable glory—only this time it was not just a glum policeman he woke to face, but total disillusion, the collapse of his dream of happiness in love. Again he did a lot he had done before, but at a much greater depth. *The tramp* had shown the pathetic, the lyrical and the rapturously joyful Charlie; *The bank* showed Charlie the tragedian.

The bank

As janitor, Charlie began his working day in a fury of trouble-making, sloshing his mop over everyone, making incredible confusion out of waste paper and a whirling fan. After the fun and games came the pathos: from afar, Charlie had long loved Edna, the typist. But the distance between them was incommensurable (as Chaplin himself said: 'Logically it was difficult to get a beautiful girl interested in a tramp. This has always been a difficulty in my films'). In *The Tramp*, he might actually aspire to Edna, the farmer's daughter: things were simpler, rosier and more pastoral out of doors. But in the hermetic, hive-like bank, where each worker had his place and protocol was strict and unalterable, he had his badge of urban drudgery (janitor's overall, mop and pail) and Edna was all too clearly beyond him, for more than distant contemplation. Until, this particular day, she brought a tie along for the cashier's birthday, and the cashier's name happened to be Charles as well; and Charlie saw the loving note from Edna and was filled with incredulous yearnings and delights and sent a similarly loving one back, with some flowers, which Edna, finding they were not from *her* Charles, merely flung away.

Flung away, Charlie found them; and of course it meant his love and incredulous yearnings were flung away at the same time; and here Chaplin mimed grief for the first time at a heartrending level. Before, he had shown pathetic disappointment, suffering that could, with a flick of shoulders and feet, be flung off and outgrown. Now he showed grief and despair beyond tears and even beyond ordinary pathos. The old actress at Keystone had wept when he mimed a comic row of children; the old sorrows of his own un-imaginably dreadful childhood still clung to his face in repose. No one could ever have doubted the potential sadness of Charlie from the beginning, or the essential melancholy of Chaplin himself. But this degree of suffering was something altogether new and on another level of feeling from the hints and moments of sadness he had shown before. In *The bank* Chaplin finally did away with the distinction between what was funny and what was sad, moving in a few minutes from riotous farce to deepest sorrow, feeling, even tragedy. Like the others, *The bank* was a two-reeler, ten or twelve minutes long. This too seems incredible when you consider its impact.

Towards the end of the day, the cashier and Edna were putting the money away when thieves burst in on them. The cowardly cashier fled, Edna was seized and gagged. Then came Charlie's chance, his moment of triumph; he whirled into the attack, rescued Edna, the money and the entire situation. The cashier was disgraced, and Charlie, triumphant, turned at last to kiss the admiring Edna . . .

He was kissing his mop; it was all a dream. Edna and the cashier were standing near him, and it was they who were doing the real-life kissing. It was the end of hope, and this time there was no twitch of final triumph, no dance to a gay horizon. Charlie just kicked away the flowers he had gathered up when Edna discarded them, and wandered away.

The bank with Edna Purviance

Of the remaining Essanay comedies, the most interesting is the hectic, high-speed, occasionally bawdy one called *Work*, sometimes known by the less stark and arresting title of *The paperhanger*. It started with Charlie between the shafts of a cart, like a rickshaw man, hauling his boss's paperhanging paraphernalia, buckets, brooms, brushes and a ladder, with the boss himself perched majestically on top of it all, first through traffic, then up and over the brow of an endless hill: endless because whenever Charlie looked like getting to the top of it something happened to haul him down again, and he was whisked into the air, legs whirling, by the weight of the stuff he was pulling. Distanced, he looked like some melancholy ant, crouched to make almost a quadruped yet with hints of human desperation about the curve of back and the twitch of elbows. A more emphatic director would have shown him in close-up for more immediate effect, sweat-gleaming face and bulging biceps. 'A close-up is a question of feeling,' Chaplin wrote. 'In some instances a long shot can effect greater emphasis.' In this case it achieves almost surrealistic effects with the circle of the hill against the sky, and the toiling, back-broken Charlie tugging the cart across an infinite horizon.

If this is social criticism, his arrival at the unlucky house where he was to do the decorating quickly dispelled all thoughts of it, because Charlie at his wildest took a wild social revenge. Paperhanging, like pie-throwing, has long been the stuff of farce, in films and out of them: there is something irresistibly ridiculous about the way the wallpaper is so delicately balanced on the end of a broom and then, with a miracle of lightfingeredness, made to stay where it ought to, on the wall. Charlie did everything with his wallpaper except stick it where it should be, and even more with his paste, which ended up all over the boss's head like foam from a fire-extinguisher or dough from an uncooked loaf, while Charlie added to the excitement while seemingly trying to soften it, sousing the poor man with water and slithering about in the resulting mess. When he came to do wallpapering on his own, he wrapped himself up in it, and when he finally disentangled himself got busy making love to the maid. This was Edna again, of course, and again, of course, Charlie was rejected.

It is in this film that Charlie had one of his famous moments of

Work with Charles Insley

business with inanimate objects, manicuring his nails with the decorator's tools, each an enormous replica of the real thing—filing them with a file a foot long, cleaning them with a trowel, buffing them with an outsize polisher of some sort. This is the kind of thing that people remember as typical of him, the brilliant set piece of comic inventiveness, like the dismembering of the clock in *The pawnshop* or the delicately eaten meal of stewed boots, with spaghetti-like laces, in *The gold rush*.

Of the other Essanay comedies, two at least (*Carmen* and *Police*) were mangled after Chaplin left Essanay, and three others put together out of films he had made for them. *The Essanay Chaplin review of 1916* and *Chase me Charlie* were simply compiled from

Carmen

his old films into, respectively, five and seven reels, but *Triple trouble*, a curious hodge-podge which Essanay claimed as a new Chaplin comedy, used material from earlier films, some of it new, and, with trick editing and doubling, a certain amount of material added in later, without Chaplin being involved with it at all.

Carmen (or *Charlie Chaplin's burlesque on Carmen*) was a burlesque of the film versions made of the opera (one by De Mille, the other a Fox version, with Theda Bara), rather than of the opera itself. Chaplin meant it to be a two-reeler, but Essanay spun it out to four reels, and Chaplin sued them for it : he had shot an enormous amount of spare material and the result of using what he never really intended to put in the finished picture is sometimes con-

Carmen with Edna Purviance

fusing and dull. But there are moments of characteristic virtuosity, particularly in the duel, which Chaplin used as an excuse for all kinds of other goings on, turning it into a dance, a game of billiards, a wrestling-match, a boring time-waster from which he could temporarily retire, and a reason for flying across the room on a string of onions hung from the ceiling. After all this, the end seemed disconcertingly dramatic, with Chaplin (as 'Darn Hosiery') killing Edna (a rather placid-looking and temperamentally un-suitable Carmen) with what looked like complete conviction, then, after a moment's pause while everyone played dead, leaping up into life again and showing the audience how easy it was to kill with an actor's knife.

Carmen with Edna Purviance

Police, Chaplin's last film for Essanay, had a sequence taken out of it and used to make up *Triple trouble*; the whole film was to some extent mangled and confused and hard to judge. A good many of its situations and gags had been used before or were to be used again. Charlie was an ex-convict persuaded to go straight until disillusion sent him back to crime; then luck, gratitude and Edna saved him from the police until, back on the road with thoughts of a rosier future, he tangled with his original enemy from the police. It was a circular tale, going back to where it started.

By the sea, an improvised one-reeler, made at the sea-side with Edna Purviance and Billy Armstrong (Charlie's fellow janitor in *The bank*); *A woman*, Chaplin's third film impersonation of a woman; *Shanghaied*, a more slapstick comedy than the other later Essanay films, involving Charlie in a plot (which he foiled) to

A woman with Charles Insley

A woman

blow up a boat for the insurance money; and *A night in the show* (also called *Charlie at the show*), which was the old skit from his Fred Karno company days, *A night in an English music hall*, in which he played a drunk (Mr Pest) in the orchestra and a gutter-snipe (Mr Rowdy) in the gallery; the sketch which had impressed Mack Sennett enough to hire Chaplin for Keystone, and therefore the beginning of all Chaplin's success on the screen; these were the rest of his Essanay films. By the time he had made them all he had far outgrown the financial possibilities of Essanay.

Mutual Film Corporation

Chaplin's next contract, with the Mutual Film Corporation, again gave him ten times what he had been getting a year earlier: $670,000 a year, or $10,000 a week and a starting bonus of $150,000. It was a long way from the days, only two years before, when $150 a week had seemed a fortune. Chaplin could never get used to the money piling up, to approaching millionairedom.

Basically more disturbing (in the sense of disconcerting, altering, upheaving) was the fame that had swept him into a totally different world from any he had known so far. He was now treated as a celebrity wherever he went—crowds turned out at railway stations, mayors made speeches of welcome, he was mobbed in restaurants and had to escape the fans in taxis; unlike Charlie, he was pursued by women as well. This is all a familiar routine today, but in Chaplin's time it was, on that scale at least, unprecedented. Perhaps more important to his way of life was the fact that he not only met the famous, the distinguished, the rich and the powerful, but was treated by them as an equal. He was now in the curious position of a man whose opinion is seriously sought on subjects he may know nothing about; and Chaplin was an artist, not (though the one does not necessarily cut out the other) an intellectual. Clearly his exchanges with intellectuals were sometimes unrewarding, the instinctive knowledge he could put across in mime being oddly muffled when it came to words. After an evening of highpowered chat with Cocteau (through an interpreter, too: 'Mr Cocteau—he say—you are a poet—of—zer sunshine—and he is a poet of zer—night') Chaplin felt he could take no more of it and spent the rest of the sea voyage they were making together slinking about the ship in order to avoid him. His description of the two distinguished fellow-voyagers (for Cocteau, it seems, felt exactly the same as Chaplin) busily escaping each other in the small space available, reading menus with furious concentration, making appointments they failed to keep, reads like the script for a comedy of manners: not, perhaps, typically Chaplinesque but highly filmable.

The fireman *and overpage* with Edna Purviance

87

Not surprisingly, the startling change in his life induced further melancholy in a man already melancholy by temperament and through the circumstances of his past, in particular those of his early life. When he came to sign the contract with Mutual, Chaplin already had the taste of ashes in his mouth, a sense of total loneliness and disillusion. 'How does one get to know people, interesting people?' he wondered. 'It seemed that everyone knew me but I knew no one.' By then, of course, people were pressing friendship upon him. Throughout his life, despite periods of intense personal unpopularity in particular places and for particular reasons, this was to continue. But friendship offered to a man because he is an artist and has done great things, or because he is successful and rich and, for all these reasons, interesting, is different *in kind* from the spontaneous, unmotivated (or scarcely motivated) relationships of unsuccessful, inartistic days. Of all the early relationships in his life only those with his brother Sydney and, of course, his much loved but unbalanced mother seem to have bridged the gap between Chaplin's old life and his new, public, alarmingly successful one. Perhaps this made them seem doubly important to him: as Sydney had touchingly written, when they were boys, and separated: 'All we have is each other. So you must write regularly and let me know that I have a brother.'

But the melancholy seems to have passed and Chaplin described the Mutual period as the happiest of his whole career. The films were made more slowly than those at Essanay, and much more carefully and soberly, of course, than the Keystone comedies; more footage was shot and discarded, more trouble taken, more time spent in planning and rehearsals and less in improvisation. Twelve comedies were made in sixteen months, 'which included time off for colds and minor impediments', Chaplin said. Edna Purviance had come across from Essanay with him, so there was a family atmosphere about the films, but the first one, *The floorwalker*, which had great popular success although by Chaplin's standards it was unremarkable, was more Keystone than Essanay

The floorwalker

in style. When Sennett saw it he wondered why, in Chaplin's Keystone days, they had never thought of using an escalator for 'business' (in *The floorwalker* it was the main source of excitement and chases).

It was set in a department store, with a manager, a floorwalker, a store detective and girls who kept asking the wandering Charlie, entranced by this or that on the counters, what he was going to buy. He looked a suspicious character in such a place, but the real villains were in fact the floorwalker and the manager, who were plotting a bolt with the takings. Then there were double-crossings between the crooks and an attempt by the floorwalker to swap clothes with Charlie, whom he looked like; and finally a wild chase up and down the escalator and in the lift. Its best moments came when Charlie and the floorwalker met and each thought he was seeing himself in a mirror: here, for a moment, was a piece of recognizably Chaplinesque fantasy, suggestive of so much else. But most of the film seems fairly perfunctory, a case of gags rather than humour, of situations rather than life itself.

The floorwalker with Albert Austin

The fireman is even more farcical and elementary, but made with enormous exuberance. Nonsense abounds. Charlie played a fireman, grotesquely unlikely in fireman's helmet, perpetually in the wrong place at the wrong time, at the wrong fire, manning the wrong hose, taking out the fire-engine when there wasn't a fire or playing checkers when there was. But in spite of it all he rescued

The fireman

Edna from a burning house which her crooked father had tried to burn down for the insurance money. Firehoses, of course, are as much the stuff of farce as wallpaper and paste and escalators and pies and banana skins. Chaplin knew better than most what to do with a jet of water, and the fantasy that could be extracted from a wriggling hose.

The fireman

Then came *The vagabond*, with Chaplin again advancing, discovering more about Charlie. After the slapstick and exuberance of *The fireman* there was little of either in *The vagabond*; indeed there were not many jokes of a sort to make you laugh outright and scarely any set pieces of routine clever business; the atmosphere was one of lyricism and light. Charlie was the tramp again, a dreamy, roving, gentle soul with a violin, chased out into the countryside by the furious members of a German band, under whose noses he had been taking a collection in a saloon bar for his own, almost unheard, violin solo. There, by a gypsy caravan, angrily beaten by an old gypsy woman of startling ugliness, he found Edna, beautiful and mysterious drudge of the gypsy band, doing the washing in a primitive washtub. Charlie came up and played his fiddle for her, tenderly cheering her up, bowing to an imaginary audience and miming applause, falling into the washtub and leaping out happily, terrified of the hag and the ferocious, whip-brandishing gypsy chief, sweetly and cunningly wooing the girl with music and jokes.

But who was Edna? Clearly not a gypsy. Far away, loving and desperate, a grey-haired woman mourned over the picture of her daughter, stolen away.

When the gypsies moved on, Charlie followed the caravan and prepared for one of his bursts of heroism. Flat on the branch of a tree he swung a club to terrible effect and as each gypsy walked below he felled him. In a moment the ground was littered with

The vagabond

gypsies and Charlie had whisked Edna into the caravan and bolted away. When morning came everything was lyrical with love and hopefulness; Charlie had slept outside (though lying on something prickly), Edna inside the caravan. But already Charlie's downfall was on its way in the shape of a handsome artist who drew Edna's portrait and won her heart. Result: at the exhibition of the portrait Edna's mother saw it, recognized her daughter and rushed out in a motor-car to find her and take her home. In the hurly-burly of reconciliation and joy they all seemed to forget Charlie, who was left standing, staring wistfully after the departing car.

This was, of course, the right ending, in tune with the image of Charlie and his vision of the world, in tune with the story and its atmosphere. But Chaplin made two more endings. The official one is happy, but it lacks conviction. Suddenly realizing it was Charlie she loved, Edna made her parents turn the car round and go back for him. But it seems Chaplin also made a private ending, in which Charlie committed suicide by jumping (twice) into the river, the first time rescued by an old woman so hideous that the sight of her made him jump straight back into the water.

The vagabond

One A.M. was a piece of virtuosity involving Chaplin the mime and the inanimate objects that surrounded and maddened him—beds, rugs, stuffed animals, staircases, doors. At one in the morning, he was dignifiedly drunk. This was unlike Chaplin's other films, particularly the other Mutuals, in that it had no story and no other characters (except for the very brief appearance of a taxi-driver at the beginning), and was a kind of pure, personal display of brilliance, a solo performance of sustained pantomime with help from no one else. In it Chaplin discarded the role of Charlie and wore evening dress.

Everything in his grotesque house (grotesque furniture was an important part of the early Chaplin films: perhaps the years between have increased our sense of its grotesqueness, and some of the objects, at the time, may have seemed more normal than they do now) combined to challenge his right and longing to get to bed. In fact, the end of the film saw him tucked up in the bath. The bed itself was a folding one that refused to accept him, and every time he thought he had conquered it, it turned round to fling him out again. It was then a case of Chaplin versus the bed, as if the horrible object had acquired a leering consciousness and must be approached and defeated with guile, crept up to, inveigled into accepting a sleeper. Of course, in the end it was the bed, not Chaplin, that won.

The count was in line with a number of other Chaplin films, the first of which was the Keystone *Her friend the bandit*, the most famous of which was *The adventurer*, in which Charlie impersonated someone grand and thus got into a party. The outsider, once inside, had the time of his life making, then covering up, mistakes, and the story gave Chaplin every excuse for demonstrating the virtuosity and dexterity (rather than the pathos and sublimity) of Charlie. It was obviously a popular theme, since Chaplin kept going back to it, and gave him the chance of using not physical but (as it were) mental disguise—impersonation—and playing all kinds of variations on themes of cunning, subterfuge, illusion, disillusion, even appearance and reality.

One A.M.

The pawnshop came next. Say 'Chaplin' to the general filmgoer and this is probably one of the films he will come back with (or at least he will probably remember the clock incident out of it). Like *One A. M.,* it was a film that seemed designed to display Chaplin's gifts for mime at their most extraordinary, within a very small physical space (no chases, no outdoors). But unlike *One A.M.* it had other characters and a story of sorts, and above all it had Charlie, not an evening-dressed Chaplin.

Charlie, as in so many other films, played an assistant, a dogs-body who did a little of everything for a boss who faintly embodied all bosses and tyrants, all unloved authority. A pawnshop is more full of objects than most places, and on any one of these objects Chaplin could improvise. Everything was usable, everything had several faces, its own and its fanciful others thought up by Chaplin, conjured from nowhere but his own peculiarly, pictorially fertile imagination. Inventiveness never went further, in any of the other comedies, than it did in this one. It does not explore or expand Charlie's soul, or give us a sense of the pathos and lyricism of the world, or of the sorrows and delights of love and hope and disillusion, as *The vagabond* does, or *The tramp,* or *The bank*. But in a series of small scenes it produces more wonders with inanimate objects, more perfect pieces of clowning with wringers and electric fans and dough and hammers and ropes and feather dusters, than any two-reeler ought, in the nature of two-reelers and objective reality, to contain. Of course, objective reality was never something that exercised Chaplin particularly. Like all artists, he was concerned with metaphor, the expansibility and elasticity and multiplicity of things, the way they could be endlessly increased and varied to make other things, the way they could suggest, hint, twist themselves into something besides themselves ; he was concerned, of course, with the underside of reality, not its top layer, its realism.

The pawnshop

Take the clock scene in *The pawnshop*. This is probably Chaplin's most famous few minutes, and deservedly so. It is not just a case of fertile inventiveness, it looks like the genius of inventiveness itself at work. Out of a mere clock in a mere few minutes Chaplin wrung so many applications and variations that one's head spins to think of them all in a row. Here was the metaphorical stretching of the plainest of objects almost to infinity, the application of one reality to another, the multiplication of life that can be done with mime and that was largely lost when mime left the cinema and more explicit forms took over from it. All this is awe inspiring, but it is also very funny.

It may seem gratuitous, almost insulting, to call Chaplin at his most brilliant 'funny'. *Of course* he is funny, some people retort indignantly; but he is not (since funniness is too personal to be universally agreed upon) universally found to be so. Sometimes, at his most brilliant, a certain hardness and brightness comes into the performance, removing the funniness which is something indefinable and warmer and tends to be lost under the sheen of perfection. But the clock scene is both perfect and funny; it makes one, like Matilda, gasp and stretch one's eyes, but agreeably so, with delight.

The clock is brought in by a shady-looking character, whom Charlie, understandably, looks at askance. Charlie then looks the clock over. He examines it as if he were a doctor, ausculating and tapping, he opens the back up with a tin-opener, hammers and prods, altering its nature with each treatment, looks at its innards as if he were a jeweller, a dentist, a plumber, removes the squirming springs and gazes at them with distaste, squirts oil over them to still their wriggling . . . then sweeps them together and hands them back, shaking his head.

Behind the screen, which came after *The pawnshop*, is slapstick to end all slapstick. It is also satire on slapstick of the Keystone kind, and particularly on the custard pie, dozens of which were thrown during the film, and landed on everything and everyone. Charlie was a kind of assistant propman, hauling and carting, banging and dropping, working at a frenzied pace to make chaos.

Behind the screen with Edna Purviance, Eric Campbell

Edna, trying to get a chance as an actress, disguised herself as a stagehand. In a well-known scene Charlie played barber to a bearskin rug, massaging and combing and wrapping a hot towel round it. Pies flew, the pace was accelerated, things grew wilder and wilder till chaos took over entirely.

Behind the screen with Eric Campbell

The rink

The rink has always been popular, being easy to take and easy on the eye. It presented no difficulties to an audience and showed Chaplin at his most obviously balletic, skilful and graceful—on roller skates: no sufferings, no disturbances, just a reassuring display of agility. In it Chaplin combined the old theme of the imposter at the party with the new situation of a party set in a roller-skating rink. Charlie played a waiter who spent his lunch-hour skating and met, and later disguised himself to meet again,

107

the roller-skating Edna. A prodigious mix-up involving Charlie with Mr and Mrs Stout, customers at his restaurant, Edna whom Mr Stout was pursuing, and the man Mrs Stout was pursuing, ended, after a tremendous free-for-all on the rink, with Charlie hooked to a car by his cane, and the rest of them still pursuing.

The rink with Edna Purviance, Eric Campbell, Albert Austin

The rink with Eric Campbell

Pages 110–111 **The cure**

Two more Mutual comedies in much the same style, and both enormously popular, are *The cure* and *The adventurer*. *The cure* took Charlie, though not in Charlie costume (he wore a light coat and a straw hat), to an hotel full of invalids and oddities taking the waters for their ailments. Revolving doors, apparently placed to catch the lame and the maimed at a disadvantage, presented no difficulty to Charlie, who spun through them with perfect freedom, pinning some bandaged unfortunate between them, however, on his way out the other side. This was rather in the style of the old 'bad-taste' Charlie, who would nick a baby's

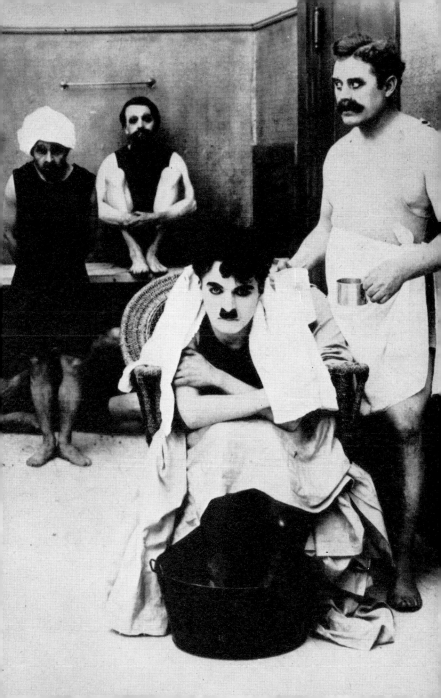

Left and above **The cure** with Edna Purviance

PITTSBURGH FILM-MAKERS INC.
P. O. BOX 7467
PITTSBURGH, PA 15213

candy or happily kick a lady in the rear. He arrived with a luggage-load of drink, which got thrown down the well the patients were drinking from, with uproarious results. He had a session in a sort of remedial gym, with masseurs and other huge official torturers. He met Edna, fell in love and dropped into the well head first. In other words, it was another slapstick mix-up, very funny in places but less endearing than some.

113

The adventurer is the comedy almost everyone appears to have seen on 8 mm., the one that always seems to turn up at children's parties and is remembered as 'typical Chaplin'. It is, of course, no more typical than the greater comedies, but it combines a good many of the old themes and gags at a high level of efficiency; in fact it seems to sum up most of what Chaplin had been doing so far in the way of slapstick and elaborate 'business'.

In a convict's horizontally-striped suit, Charlie was on the run from the police. By the seashore, scrambling up cliffs, plunging down holes, his head popping out just when a policeman was

Opposite **The adventurer**

The cure with Henry Bergman

The adventurer with Albert Austin

passing, his breakneck course took him round policemen, between policemen, and diving down among policemen's legs till their heads spun. Fantastic escapes took place on cliff-paths, beaches, caves, chases in which Charlie seemed to be leading some joyous dance across the sands, with policemen streaming behind him; or he would watch their incompetent clumsiness from some hiding place, chortling with glee. The timing of it all was extraordinary, but no longer surprising.

Then came the adventure proper: Charlie rescued Edna from drowning, and since by now he had shed his convict's outfit and was wearing a stolen swimsuit, things began to look brighter. In his new character he was invited to a party at Edna's where he put his foot in it and retrieved it at breakneck speed—flinging his arms up when a champagne cork popped, then quickly smoothing down his hair to cover the mistake and make the movement look natural, for instance. A splendid, though contrived, piece of business occurred when Charlie's ice-cream slipped down his trouser-leg, through the grill floor of the balcony he was sitting on, and shot down the back of Edna's mother's evening dress, on the balcony below. Chaplin has explained the psychology of discomfiture as illustrated in this incident: an ice cream dropped down a poor woman's back would have outraged the audience, but a rich, dressed up, well-fed woman, able to afford her own party, was fair game for minor insults of the kind.

But Charlie's luck could hardly hold forever. Edna's jealous suitor saw a newspaper photograph of Charlie the escaped convict and in no time at all the house was overrun with chasing policemen. A final delicate touch came when Charlie grabbed a lampshade, put it on his head and froze into a kind of caryatid as they all streamed past.

Two more films, both famous, both more serious in content than the later slapsticks, both more closely linked than the rest with Chaplin's own past of poverty and deprivation, complete the list of those he made for Mutual in 1916 and '17: *Easy Street* and *The immigrant*.

Easy Street has long been something of a puzzle. The outcast Charlie 'reforms' and joins the police; this seems not just improbable but impossible. Then the whole thing savours of a curiously directed satire, but one cannot always tell just where it is directed, nor what Chaplin's mood was in directing it. The film started with Charlie at his most tramp-like wandering into a mission, pinching the collection box, seeing Edna and instantly reforming and returning it. Then, in the middle of much street brawling, in which the police were at their wits' end, he decided to join the force—but on his own terms. First there was the local bully to settle, an enormous fellow who spurned the minute new policeman in his outsize helmet, but was first puzzled by his antics in a telephone box, then made to put his head inside a street gaslamp, so that Charlie could turn on the gas and asphyxiate him into surrender. Other sociologically impressive things happened, including the famous scene in which Charlie fed a brood of children as if they were chickens, and another in which, Robin Hood-like, he pinched vegetables from a well-provided barrow for a woman who seemed to have none. Then came some hanky-panky from a gang of anarchists and drug takers, who accidentally injected Charlie (when he banged on the hypodermic needle) with massive doses of toughness and courage. Under his dapper leadership Easy Street, including even its huge bully (now out of the gas-lamp), reformed, and the subtitle told us that:

> 'Love backed by Force,
> Forgiveness sweet,
> Bring Hope and Peace
> To Easy Street.'

In social matters, Chaplin has always been something of a mystery; his social attitudes are not easily summarized, and this ambivalence of his towards such things as riches and poverty, power and powerlessness, are reflected in the slightly ambiguous quality of even a fairly light-hearted film like *Easy Street*. Chaplin

Easy Street

Pages 120–121 **The immigrant**

can never be called fully left-wing nor is he, needless to say, politically right-wing; he was, of course, taken over by the world's left, particularly in his early days, as a symbol of much that Charlie seemed to represent. On the other hand, as *Easy Street* already makes clear and as Chaplin was to confirm unambiguously in his *Autobiography*, he was totally opposed to the sentimentalized idea of himself as an advocate of poverty and the simple life as being somehow more 'real', therefore artistically more valuable, than a life in which freedom, including artistic freedom, could be bought with money. Somerset Maugham, of all people, wrote a highly sentimentalized account of Chaplin the lost Cockney, perpetually seeking 'real life' in the outward signs of poverty, and suffering, throughout a life of physical ease, from 'nostalgia for the slums'. This irritated Chaplin enormously: 'I have yet to know a poor man who has nostalgia for poverty,' he snapped.

Easy Street with Janet Miller Sully, John Rand

The immigrant with Eric Campbell, Edna Purviance. Henry Bergman

The immigrant was more directly personal in tone and autobiographical in spirit than *Easy Street*, and the result was denser and deeper than that of any of Chaplin's films so far. Of all his early work it came closest to his darker and more directly satirical films of the late twenties and thirties. Charlie played a part that suited him not just on the surface, but in his whole personality: he was an immigrant, an outsider, a non-belonger in the great society, entering the States with other immigrants as poor and displaced as himself, all herded together like cattle as the ship passed the Statue of Liberty—which Charlie glanced at quizzically. Edna and her mother were immigrants too, and for once Charlie got his girl, but after vicissitudes that scarcely made it seem a 'happy ending' in the abrupt, conventional sense of the word. The plot of the story in the second half of the film, when Edna's mother had died and she and Charlie had met again, turned on a coin which passed through several hands and pockets and was at last found to be a fake. Love, security, marriage and hope, were all finally achieved, but the mood was one of solemnity rather than rapture. It was all a very long way from Keystone or even the more sophisticated but still Keystone-type comedy—*The adventurer*—to which he turned next, and which finished his contract with Mutual.

Chaplin had always toyed with the theme of the outsider, and in *The immigrant* was simply highlighting the 'outcast' aspect of Charlie's nature. The tramp is an eternal outsider to ordinary society, the immigrant an outsider compared with the native, and Chaplin himself was not merely an immigrant in America—how precariously poised there, later events were to show—but an immigrant in the entire society to which, with success, he had suddenly climbed. For a climber, however much welcomed, never belongs, and there is always a certain selfconciousness even about his welcome: on his first visit to London, at every dinner party Chaplin attended, including a grand occasion at the Garrick, where a large number of men distinguished in the arts and literature had gathered to honour him, and a private dinner with a man as (apparently) sensitive as Sir Philip Sassoon, he was given treacle pudding because he had been quoted as saying he was coming back to find the treacle pudding of his boyhood. If Maugham's idea of his 'nostalgia for the slums' was irritating, this

125

slightly more sophisticated mania for sentimentalizing Chaplin's past must have scratched at least the surface of his composure, of his sense of belonging, each time it happened. The patronage of treacle pudding was often to be his lot.

The immigrant with Edna Purviance

The First National

Chaplin was now working much more slowly: he no longer needed to be whipped into activity by fear of failure, poverty or his studio bosses. During 1918 and '19 he made three films for the First National: *A dog's life, Shoulder arms* and *Sunnyside*.

A dog's life made a parallel, as Chaplin himself said, between the life of a tramp and the life of a dog. Charlie was no longer the joyous vagabond wandering the countryside and meeting charming gypsy girls or farmers' daughters: he was a desperate beggar with a dog as beggarly, whose search for a job was frustrated by others as desperate as himself, just as his dog's search for a bone was frustrated but by other dogs as hungry. In his *Autobiography* Chaplin quotes Conrad as saying that life made him feel like a cornered blind rat waiting to be clubbed, and adds: 'This simile could well describe the appalling circumstances of us all.' Chaplin knew nothing about the happy vagabond's life except what he imagined and what he learnt from the happy vagabond in San Francisco. He had not the time, the inclination or the temperament to go slumming: once he was rich, he lived a rich man's life, hobnobbing with other rich men—Hearsts, Fairbanks, Sassoons. But from his own past he knew what it was to be a beggar, to sell flowers or his mother's last rags in the street, to be tormented at school for wearing her cut-down tights (as his brother wore her cut-down high-heeled shoes, an even worse torment), to be sent to that lowest circle of Victorian hell, the workhouse, to have his head shaved, to be cold, hungry, dirty, whipped, and to have to cope, almost in infancy, with adults who are drunk, mad or desperate. This he knew all too closely, and it all went into the portrait, not of a sentimentalized tramp, not of a poetic tramp, and certainly no longer of a happy or lyrical tramp, but of a man living in the sort of poverty that has no lyricism about it. But it could still have jokes.

Charlie lay beside a fence, hoping to keep out the wind, but the fence was full of holes which he tried to stuff up, not too successfully. When a policeman looked over the fence at him he

A dog's life (*Pages 128–131*)

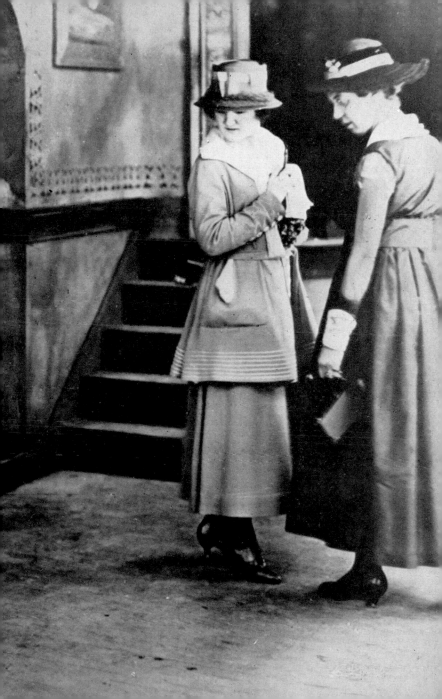

rolled under it, when the policeman looked back on the other side he rolled back to where he had been. At last he tied the policeman's shoe-laces together, a solution as neat as the suffragettes' reputed habit of cutting policemen's braces.

In a cabaret he met Edna, of course, leading another sort of dog's life from which, when a hope of money came to him, he might be able to rescue her. The money was found by his dog in a wallet hidden by those who originally took it and were now determined to keep it. As in other films (sometimes merely in dreams) Charlie took on any number of enemies at once, so now he battled with the thieves and came out of it triumphant. But the triumph was steeped in sadness. His films had often ended with a walk down the road: now he walked off with Edna and dog, but it seemed no more conclusive.

A dog's life

Shoulder arms was a war-film made during that dangerous time for war-films, wartime itself. Friends warned Chaplin against making it. De Mille said: 'It's dangerous at this time to make fun

Shoulder arms

of the war.' And, as everyone knew, Chaplin had not been in the army himself (and had had his share of criticism for it), so that he might be thought incompetent to make pronouncements about

Shoulder arms *and pages 136–137*

army life. As it turned out, the people whose opinion really counted—the soldiers themselves—were enthusiastic; but at first Chaplin himself felt downcast about it, and infected the rest of the

Shoulder arms

studio with his own depression. It was his close friend Douglas
Fairbanks Senior who stopped him scrapping it. He saw it and
laughed without stopping, except for fits of coughing. 'Sweet

Shoulder arms

Douglas, he was my greatest audience,' Chaplin remarked. So it went ahead.

Charlie was a soldier; but again, as he had been a policeman, on his own terms. Chaplin originally meant to show Charlie's life before he joined up and after the war, but decided against it and stuck to the wartime middle of the story. As a soldier, then, Charlie seemed to have no background and no future, nothing but the grey present of French trenches, mud, rain and occasional vengeful fun with mousetraps. He seemed to get no letters and his one parcel turned out to be a malicious joke, full of dog-biscuits. At one point he nearly sank into the watery trench for-ever, neatly smoothing out his pillow in the muddy water and lying down in it. He was perpetually being ordered to attack, and frustrated in his efforts to do so; but dressed up as a tree he was rather more successful. The tree episode was one of Chaplin's happiest: everyone could expect Charlie to tumble over his own feet at drill, to mangle the smartness of a line of recruits or to fly down ladders into trenches. But to be—to *become*—a tree was a triumph of comic impersonation. '*Shoulder arms* was made in the middle of a sizzling heatwave,' Chaplin wrote. 'Working inside a camouflaged tree . . . was anything but comfortable.' The effect of damp, dreary, non-Californian weather is perfect, all the same, and very much at one with the long overcoats, long whiskers, European formalities.

Shoulder arms

Today, when there have been attempts to make comic films about the Second World War, *Shoulder arms* stands up better than ever. Jokes made *at the time*, dangerous jokes, thin-ice and possibly-bad-taste jokes, came across with perfect rightness, richness and point. As they still do. A serious film on a modern war would have to be like modern war itself: therefore unviewable, impossible to take. Chaplin, as ever, went to the underside of the business, skimming beneath the unbearable top layer to the tragi-comic, hilarious, just-bearable layer of laughter and bitterness. It was an extraordinary imaginative feat for a man who had no personal experience of war, or even of the rigours and jokes of army life, of what was acceptable to men in such conditions, and what wasn't.

Shoulder arms

Sunnyside was back in peacetime, and the most peaceable and lyrical of all Chaplin's films. Yet he describes making it as being 'like pulling teeth'. Personal problems (his first marriage—to Mildred Harris) had had their effect on his mind but not on the final result of his work, which seemed supremely effortless; in fact, it is hard to consider effort at all in relation to a work of this kind. Charlie played a farmworker, again antagonistic to his boss, again in love with Edna; cowman and dogsbody and general run-about for a hard task-master. The story mattered little—though for the record Charlie seemed to get his girl, the rival who came to make him suffer turning out to be only a dream. Dreams of escape, heroism or dread all played their part in Chaplin's films; but the centre of *Sunnyside* was an idyllic dream in which Chaplin, coatless, hatless and therefore less recognizably Charlie than usual, with a flower in his hair, danced about the meadow with four girls in Greek tunics who turned up from nowhere and led him on to dance with them. That was all. There was, of course, a pinch of satirical intention about it, but it matters very little at this distance. What counts is Charlie, not only at his most balletic (he was balletic, but much more rigorously, soullessly so in *The rink*), but at his most lyrical and other-worldly, in a mood that might be described as one of total dance, abandon and poetry.

W. C. Fields called Chaplin 'the greatest ballet dancer that ever lived', but a greater compliment to his art came from the man who was probably just that: Nijinsky. Six months before he went mad Nijinsky asked Chaplin to his dressing room and made gauche, banal conversation which evidently mattered supremely to him because he kept the audience waiting while overtures were re-played and he continued his inconsequential talk with Chaplin. 'Let them wait, this is more interesting,' he said. One is reminded, a little, of the meeting between Chaplin and Cocteau, only this time the roles were reversed, it was Chaplin who was the more worldly, embarrassed at Nijinsky's inability to communicate what apparently was pressing on his mind—admiration and fellow-feeling. Chaplin described Nijinsky then, at their single meeting, as 'a sensitive mind on its way out of a brutal war-torn world into another of its own dreaming'. This might stand as a description

Sunnyside with Edna Purviance

Sunnyside

of *Sunnyside*: only Chaplin did not crack like Nijinsky. His was the sort of mind to bend and stand upright again: his was the therapy, which Nijinsky lacked, of laughter.

Before his success . . .   and after

Postscript

So, nearly half a century ago, Chaplin ended his early period, the run of one-, two- and three-reelers that established him as actor and director and made his creation, Charlie, a part of modern mythology, at once famous and familiar. Remote as the legends that grew up around him yet, like any well-worn, long-established fictional character, seeming reassuringly close as well, Charlie was in the odd position of any artist's creation who, through the years, is in a sense extended autobiographically, yet never loses his own presence and individuality, is never taken over by his creator. Inevitably, he was confounded with Chaplin; inevitably, as Chaplin's own life drew further away from its origins—which had produced Charlie, and in which Charlie continued to live—the contrast between the two seemed more marked : piquant to some, irritating and even dislikable to others. For a mixture of personal and political reasons too complex to go into here, while Charlie has been much loved, Chaplin has been much hated, much persecuted ; and while Charlie has crossed the barriers of race and nationality, Chaplin has, for the last third of his life at least, been exiled to that cosmopolitan no-man's-land, Switzerland, as earlier success and money exiled him from his birthplace and the early life on which he continued to draw for his inspiration in developing Charlie. The relationship between Chaplin and Charlie, who is basically the only fictional character on which he has concentrated (which is like saying a novelist spent fifty years developing a single character through endless fictional situations and with endless variations), in the deepest sense Charlie's autobiographical content, or perhaps function, is endlessly mysterious, a source of circular speculation, fascinating but insoluble, and efforts to explain either entirely in terms of the other are bound to fail, since the two overlap, yet neither contains the other.

Chaplin's earliest comedies, at Keystone, were made with astonishing speed, and so, necessarily, without much preparation or revision. As he advanced, his methods slowed down, gradually at first, then much more noticeably. From a lightning artist he became a deliberate one, endlessly preparing and re-making, shooting perhaps a hundred times the amount of film he would finally use. From a haphazard social critic who implied, in his stories of tramp-life, that the world was not socially ideal, he became a concentrated satirist of particular men and events and systems, politicians like Hitler and Mussolini, modern industrialism, capitalism. He still insisted that he was non-political, that his aim was to entertain and not to make statements, that he was merely laughing at politicians as he had previously laughed at policemen or large men with beards or stout ladies; but politics, of course, merely means the translation of attitudes and Chaplin's attitudes, though confused, were plain enough. In the hysterical atmosphere of the cold war in the late forties and fifties it was probably inevitable that he should be called a communist.

Throughout the films, from *The kid*, the first feature-length film Chaplin directed. onwards, Charlie persisted, varying as so versatile a creature might be expected to, sometimes more lyrical or more pathetic than others, sometimes madder, sometimes older, sometimes tougher, fiercer, more or less sympathetic; sometimes as a kind of alter ego to the familiar Charlie (as happened in *The great dictator*, in which he played two parts, the normal Charlie-character and the devilish Adenoid Hynkel—Adolf Hitler—who happened, in real as well as film life, to look so disconcertingly like Charlie). Even the familiar Charlie, in any case, developed and sharpened with the years. Chaplin had long been afraid of Charlie's sweetness and popularity, of the tender hold he had on people's affections. He could never stay at that touching level of public favour—the sort of popularity that came to him for a film like *The kid*, in which Charlie's nature was so extraordinarily reflected in a five-year-old and the relationship between them was not so much that of man and boy as of past and present, Charlie's (and Chaplin's) past coming up with autobiographical exactness in the shape of a ragged urchin.

In the early films Charlie had plenty of roles, plenty of jobs and even disguises. He was not always, or officially, a tramp. These roles, jobs and disguises were extended, as Charlie moved on. In *The kid* he went back to the days of trampish anti-social occupations: he was a mender of windows the Kid had first been sent ahead to shy stones through. In *City lights* he was the tramp more or less pure and simple and the beautiful girl was made interested in him through the simple device of being made blind. In *The pilgrim* he was an escaped convict, as he had been in *The adventurer*, but this time, for further complexities of plot and feeling, he was disguised as a clergyman. In *The circus* and *Limelight* he played what Chaplin himself knew best, an entertainer. In *The gold rush*, probably the most famous of all his films, he went out into the Yukon made so heroically famous by Jack London, and cooked his boots with the air of an Escoffier, delicately disposing of the nails as if they were bones and coiling the laces like spaghetti. In *Modern times* he was the industrial worm who turned by rejecting industrial society in madness. In *Monsieur Verdoux*, made twenty years ago and perhaps twenty years too soon for general understanding, he was the capitalist worm who turned on capitalist society by taking its principles to the extreme of mass murder.

The degree to which Charlie had been taken to heart by Chaplin's public, and identified with Chaplin himself, was clear in the anger aroused, and the bitter vendetta that followed it, when *Monsieur Verdoux* shattered, once and for all, the image of an autobiographical Charlie whom it was possible to love with uncomplicated amusement. For here Charlie not only discarded his costume but became a murderer of all too credible horror, who picked a worm delicately off the path to avoid stepping on it and scolded his little boy for pulling the cat's tail. Until the Second World War many people had a comfortable feeling that gentleness to animals and children was a guarantee of basic goodheartedness, but, as we have since learned that the concentration camp guards, far from being ferocious devils in private life, were often, like Monsieur Verdoux, model family men who loved their children and their cats and sang Christmas carols and lullabies, it is now impossible to equate evil with obvious ferocity. *Monsieur Verdoux* came too soon for the shocks of such revelations to have been absorbed and healthily reapplied to everyday life; it outraged Charlie's sentimental public by presenting a non-violent, delicate, all-too-recognizable murderer easily moved to liking and pity, easily moving his audience, even, to liking and pity. It even suggested unspeakable horrors in the person of Charlie's creator. It seemed, though

151

in fact it was not, an unbridgeable distance from the world of *Charlie in the park* or *The vagabond*.

But in fact Charlie's growth was implicit in the early Charlie, tough and anarchical, delicate and disciplined, furiously, seriously, sometimes desperately funny. It was this early Charlie that went round the world and established his own mythology, without pretentiousness and certainly without the modern build-up of advance publicity. It is this early Charlie most people mean when they say Chaplin.

List of Chaplin's early films, with release dates

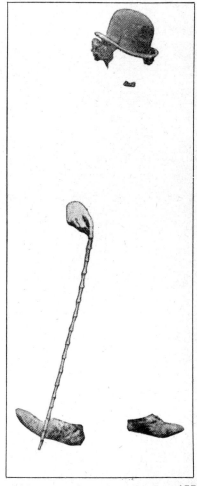

1914 (Keystone)

1915 (Essanay)

February	His new job 63
	A night out 63
March	The champion 63, 65
April	The Jitney elopement 65
	The tramp 68, 74, 75, 76
	By the sea 84
June	Work (The paperhanger) 78
July	A woman 84
August	The bank 74
October	Shanghaied 84
November	A night in the show 85

1916 March	Police 81, 84
April	Carmen 81, 82

1918

(released by Essanay
after Chaplin had left)

August	Triple trouble 82, 84

1916 (Mutual)

May	The floorwalker 90
June	The fireman 94
July	The vagabond 96
August	One A.M. 101
September	The count 101
October	The pawnshop 81, 102
November	Behind the screen 105
December	The rink 107

1917 January	Easy Street 117
April	The cure 109
June	The immigrant 117, 125
October	The adventurer 101, 109, 114

1918 (First National)